BETTER TOGETHER

BETTER TOGETHER:
EMBRACING THE DISCOMFORT OF DIFFERENCE

REGGIE DAVIS

First Printing, 2025

Dedication

"And let us consider how we may spur one another on toward love and good deeds."
— Hebrews 10:24 (NIV)

Growing up in the church, I often heard the lyrics of that old song: "We've come this far by faith." And truly, I have. But I've also come this far by the love, support, and investment of family, friends, and community who believed in me even when I didn't always believe in myself.

I dedicate this book to:

My parents, Alexander and Fannie Dean
You instilled in me not only a belief in God but also a belief in people. Your example of unwavering faith, sacrificial love, and tireless service shaped who I am. You gave your children everything you had, and then some. Yet you still managed to give just as much to others. Thank you!

My wife, Kim, and our daughters–Sydney, Kendall, and Ella
Four amazing women who have taught me more about myself—the good, the bad, and the ugly—than I ever imagined. Kim, you took a chance on a young man still living with his parents twenty-five years ago (there's a whole book in that story alone), and I'd like to believe it's paid off for both of us. Your love and partnership mean the world to me. Girls, thank you for sharpening me with your honesty, laughter, and grace. You are my heart.

My bonus parents, Charles and Ronnie Barnes
You've been more than I could have ever hoped for in in-laws. Since my father's passing in 2016, you have filled a space I didn't even know could be filled—with kindness, wisdom, and steady presence. You have been what I needed and more.

To **everyone else** who has poured into my journey: I see you, I feel you, and I carry you in these pages. I can't name you all here, but I pray this is just the first of many opportunities to uplift you. After all, UpLift starts with U (you).

With love and gratitude,
Reggie Davis

Forward by Courtney Robertson

When I think of my friend, brother, and mentor Reggie Davis, the word that comes to mind first is courage. Not the kind of courage that makes headlines or demands the spotlight, but the quieter, deeper courage that is willing to be vulnerable, to stretch, and to keep showing up for humanity in all its complexity.

I've had the privilege of walking alongside Reggie for many years. I have watched him navigate the challenges of being a husband, a father to three beautiful daughters, a pastor, an entrepreneur, and a relentless advocate for all people. What makes Reggie extraordinary is not that he wears all these titles so well, but that he consistently leads with humility and love. He leans into the difficult, the uncomfortable, and the unfamiliar - because he believes, deeply, that our shared humanity is worth the effort.

This book is Reggie's first, but it feels like it has been writing itself in him for a lifetime. Reggie invites us to journey with him from comfort zones that feel safe but stifling, into the stretching places where growth happens, and toward the joy of truly seeing and valuing one another across differences. He writes not as a distant expert but as a fellow traveler who has stumbled, learned, and continued going and growing. His stories are honest, tender, and raw. They remind us that change rarely comes without discomfort, and that discomfort is not something to fear, but to embrace.

One story in particular touches me deeply: how our friendship helped him discover greater empathy, respect, and love for a community. For both of us - Black men committed to making the world more just, compassionate, and whole - that kind of learning is not theoretical. It's personal. And it's powerful.

In a time when division is easier than dialogue, and when differences are often weaponized rather than embraced, Reggie's voice is necessary. This book is not just about "getting along" or tolerating one another. It is about pressing into the beautifully hard and complex work of connection beyond similarities. It is about seeing the image of God, the spark of humanity, in every single person. It is about choosing love when fear would be easier.

I could not be prouder of Reggie for putting these words on paper for offering his wisdom, his stories, and his heart to the world. And I am humbled to contribute to his vision. My hope is that as you read this book, you don't just nod along in agreement but allow yourself to be stretched. Let the discomfort do its work. And then, take the next step toward someone who is different from you, with open hands and an open heart.

We are, truly, better together. And Reggie Davis has given us a roadmap for how to embrace and live that truth.

Contents

Introduction: Differences on Display

***"We are caught in an inescapable network of mutuality, tied in a single garment of destiny. What affects one directly, affects another indirectly."* - Dr. Martin Luther King Jr.**

The year 2016 marked a significant moment in the history of the United States of America. On July 5, 2016, Alton Sterling was shot and killed by a police officer in Baton Rouge, LA. The next day on July 6, 2016, Philando Castile was shot and killed by a police officer in Minneapolis, MN. The deaths sparked intense national debate and highlighted differences of opinions on policing, race, and justice in the United States.

In the wake of the deaths of Alton Sterling and Philando Castile, Americans responded in deeply divided ways. Some saw these incidents as clear examples of racial bias and excessive force by law enforcement. Others interpreted them as officers responding to perceived threats in the line of duty. While many viewed the victims as compliant and unfairly targeted, others believed their actions justified the officers' responses. The tragedy in Dallas, where five police officers (Lorne Ahrens, Michael Krol, Michael Smith, Brent Thompson, and Patricio Zamarripa) were killed by a veteran expressing anger over police shootings of black men, further intensified the national con- versation. Cries of "Black Lives Matter" echoed across cities, while others rallied behind "Blue Lives Matter," reflecting the emotional and ideological divide. Across the country, people expressed a wide range of emotions - grief, anger, fear, and frustration, both in the streets and online.

For some, protests were a necessary outcry against injustice; while for others, they stirred anxiety and concern. While many mourned the loss of Black lives at the hands of police, others focused on defending law enforcement and maintaining public order. Some communities stood in solidarity with the black community's call for justice and equity, while others expressed fatigue and skepticism toward the broader conversation on systemic racism.

Often, two things can be true at once. While most law enforcement officers uphold high professional standards, instances of misconduct can occur among some individuals in the profession. Most law enforcement officers serve with integrity and professionalism. But like in any profession, there are individuals whose actions fall short, and when that happens, it can cause real harm and erode trust. It is important to recognize that individuals should not be judged based on race. While some Black men, like individuals from any demographic group, have committed crimes, it is inaccurate and unjust to associate criminality or societal threat with an entire population.

In a world that often seeks uniformity, differences can feel uncomfortable. Difference can divide families, friendships, churches, cities, and countries. Yet, it is through difference and especially our willingness to engage our differences that we grow, innovate, and truly connect. This workbook is a journey into embracing the discomfort of difference, not as a hurdle, but as a path to becoming Better Together.

The Comfort Zone - A Safe Yet Limiting Space

***"Our whole life is set up in the path of least resistance... So, the whole time, we're living our lives in a very comfortable area. There's no growth in that." –* David Goggins**

Following the murders of Sterling and Castile, a significant, nonviolent protest took place in Memphis. The protest took place on the Hernando de Soto Bridge, which connects West Memphis, Arkansas, with Memphis, Tennessee, serving as a link between the eastern and western United States. I didn't join the protest, but as I watched it on TV, I became more curious. I checked social media for different perspectives and found the comments disappointing rather than surprising.

Some friends were upset by the protests and unrest following widely publicized injustices, while others were angered both by the deaths of Mr. Castille and Mr. Sterling and by a broader history of racial injustice in the U.S., an issue that disproportionately affects people of color. Opinions on these events largely aligned with race. Discussing race remains one of America's most challenging and uncomfortable social issues, often prompting visible discomfort in diverse groups.

Understanding comfort is important when learning to embrace discomfort. Although comfort has its place, it should not be our main goal or a key measure of success. Significant success is infrequently achieved within a state of comfort.

So, what is comfort? Simply put, comfort is a state of ease. It is freedom from pain, stress, or restraint. But like most things in life, comfort becomes more complex when viewed through the lens of human experience. What feels comfortable to one person may feel unfamiliar or even unsettling to another. As a father of three daughters - raised in the same home, by the same parents, with the same extended family, worship experiences, and early education - I've come to realize that comfort looks different for each of them. And as they continue to grow and evolve, so do their definitions of comfort. Their needs shift, their thresholds change, and what once brought ease may no longer do so. Comfort, it turns out, is deeply personal and constantly evolving.

People often organize their lives to prioritize comfort, including factors like convenience, safety, and predictability. These aspects frequently become priorities in response to living in an "Either-Or" world. An "Either-Or" world thrives on simplicity: good or bad, safe or dangerous, right or wrong, us or them. This binary thinking can feel safe because it narrows down the complexity of life into categories we can easily process. It removes the discomfort of nuance. An "Either-Or" world also pushes us toward a constant prioritization of what feels comfortable, familiar or affirming, while rejecting or avoiding what feels challenging, different, or disruptive. The irony is that real life is rarely "Either-Or." It's almost always "Both-And." We can pursue comfort and still engage discomfort.

I believe that most human beings tend to gravitate toward conditions that minimize effort, reduce risk, and provide certainty more than we recognize. Let's call it unconscious comfortability. Unconscious comfortability is the subtle, almost automatic inclination to seek environments, relationships, and routines that feel familiar, safe, and effortless. This is shaped by individual experiences, environmental factors, and innate survival instincts.

To clarify, I do not consider comfort to be inherently negative. Like many positive aspects of life, comfort warrants careful attention. It is advisable to assess it periodically, perhaps by applying the 80/20 Rule of Self-awareness. This is the awareness that even a strength or talent in our life may be very valuable 80% of the time, but 20% of the time we need to manage it, or it can be or become invaluable. For example, I am naturally a people-pleaser. My friend, Eli Morris, best described a people-pleaser as someone who enjoys seeing people be happy. A people pleaser enjoys helping others be their best and fulfilled self. As someone who has spent more than 20 years in ministry and the nonprofit sector, being a people pleaser is great 80% of the time, but 20% of the time I have had to learn (and I'm still learning) to manage it. In wanting the best for others, it requires me to say or do things that might create discomfort for the other person or even myself. With this in mind, it might be easier to understand why these components of the comfort zone - convenience, safety, and predictability - become priorities in our life.

Convenience can reduce the amount of time and effort needed for certain tasks, enabling individuals to allocate attention to other activities. Achieving greater convenience often involves the use of additional tools and resources to simplify processes. In many cases, the opportunity cost for convenience is human investment and/or human interaction. When we choose the comfort of convenience, we may diminish personal effort and resilience, or we suffer the loss of deeper engagement.

An undeniable, universal component of comfort is safety. Safety is a basic need of most human beings. Safety provides peace of mind and a sense of control over one's environment. This approach enables us to safeguard both ourselves and our loved ones from potential or actual harm, risk, and danger. In our efforts to provide safety we often design environments and routines to diminish risk or eliminate threats, real or perceived. What we might lose when choosing the comfort of safety is curiosity and creativity which leads to growth.

Likewise, predictability is our human attempt to provide consistent, expected outcomes by creating systems and routines. It reduces uncertainty and the mental energy required to navigate new situations. Predictability reduces anxiety and creates a sense of stability whether it is real or perceived. It's particularly appealing in times of stress or upheaval. To experience the com- fort of predictability, we might not experience new ideas, perspectives, and experiences.

Taken together, while comfort in its various forms - convenience, safety, and predictability - offers undeniable value in our daily lives, these very elements can quietly impose limitations that prevent us from realizing our full potential. While comfort, in terms of convenience, safety, and predictability, offers significant benefits, it may not maximize an individual's potential. Comfort should not be misconstrued as a lack of diligence or care, nor is it inherently associated with complacency. Nevertheless, remaining within one's comfort zone seldom fosters personal development. Comfort can lead to a life without passion, purpose, and a genuine love for others. For sustained growth, innovation, and meaningful engagement, individuals are encouraged to challenge themselves beyond familiar boundaries.

Our pursuit of comfort can slowly suffocate the spaces where we aim to grow. Our desire for comfort can creep in quietly, subtle and undetected, until it begins to choke us like carbon monoxide: invisible, odorless, and dangerously suffocating.

Imagine participating in a conversation with an idea or comment that is burning in your heart, but you choose not to speak up. Not because the idea is irrelevant or invaluable but because you are not sure how it will be received. Moments like this are comfort checks. Comfort might look like avoiding a hard conversation with a friend or teammate, not because you don't care, but because you're afraid of rocking the boat. Or it shows up when you scroll past an article that challenges your world-view because you don't want to deal with the discomfort it might provoke. These are small decisions, often unconscious, but over time they form a pattern. Unfortunately, a pattern of comfort can become a cage that limits your ability to develop.

Comfort can create a false sense of security that blocks challenges and limits personal growth. It is important to acknowledge where comfort could be holding you back. Once you can acknowledge the comfort zones that are limiting you, you will gain the power to make different choices. Choices should be guided by a commitment to progress rather than self-preservation, fostering transformation instead of stagnation.

We grow up in families and communities with people who have had significant influence in our lives. Although individuals such as parents, grandparents, teachers, coaches, and religious leaders have dedicated themselves to our development, they have also contributed to the formation of our comfort zones. Our beliefs are often shaped by the beliefs of these influential individuals. These beliefs frequently serve as guard rails defining our comfort zones. This was certainly true in my life. I was raised in a Christian household in a small Arkansas town and naturally tend to avoid risk. My upbringing took place within a conservative community and state, with "conservative" referring to lifestyle rather than political orientation. This approach to life became an unexamined comfort zone for me, ultimately shaping my behavior to align with my surroundings, as is common among humans.

I often found comfort in following the rules. It didn't matter if I agreed with the rule or if the rule was unjust, following the rules was comfortable. For example, we had a swimming pool in our town that had a private fence around it that I did not have access to because I was black. I think back to the comfort zone that was created around the unspoken culture of segregation in our town even into the 1990's. It was not until my freshman year in college that I realized that what we deemed to be normal – a swimming pool that only white people could enjoy – was not everyone else's normal. In my Freshman Composition course, we were assigned a paper requiring us to reflect on and write about a personal experience from our past. I decided to write about my inability to swim, which stems from not having access to a swimming pool since the only one in town was private. When I finished reading my paper and saw the expressions on the faces of my classmates and the professor, I realized that I was part of a community who was comfortable with the current state or at least not willing to engage in a discussion about the swimming pool. The unspoken rule was comfortable, and my community dared not discuss or disrupt it.

The Comfort Zone ***Key Points***

◈ Choosing what is safe and familiar reduces risk and gives us a sense of control - even when it limits growth.

◈ When we prioritize comfort, we miss opportunities to grow, build resilience, and discover new possibilities.

◈ Recognizing moments when comfort is holding you back is significant.

◈ Exercise: List three areas in life where you feel "too comfortable." Reflect on what growth might look like if you stepped out of those zones. Choose one of the three areas of comfort that you can commit to do deeper work around, over the next 21 days.

____

____

____

____

____

____

Comfort to Discomfort - Overcoming Being Good

***"Growth is uncomfortable; you have to embrace the discomfort if you want to expand."* – Jonathan Majors**

A few days after the deaths of these human beings, both civilians and officers of different races, protests and online posts continued, leaving me to wonder about their impact. People who shared the same perspective were listening to each other but very few people were listening to those who had a different perspective. I had relationships with people along the whole spectrum of this challenging moment and understood that individuals on opposite sides of what was happening considered themselves to be good people and had a desire to be good. I had an idea that I believed could make the situation better, even if only minimally. I understood it could go wonderfully well or horribly bad. Through a post on social media, I invited people interested in having a healthy conversation about the racial tension in our country to meet me at a designated place, date, and time. I was hoping that maybe 15-20 people would show up and much to my surprise and joy, more than 100 people showed up. Over 100 people were willing to embrace discomfort.

The curious and courageous individuals who showed up that evening were uncertain whether others would share their perspective. They were not sure if openly sharing their thoughts and beliefs would be received well or if their perspectives would be welcomed. Perhaps they even imagined being prematurely judged as someone other than a good person. Some may call a moment like this, the fear of the unknown, but I would like to say these individuals leaned into the "discomfort of the unknown."

I believe most people desire to be regarded as good. The idea of being recognized as kind brings a sense of assurance. The prospect of being seen as ethical is comforting. Being known as fair and open-minded can also be comforting. However, striving to be perceived as good can create tension within us. When our values, beliefs, or behaviors - what we associate with our own goodness - are challenged, it can feel like who we are is at stake. Discomfort arises when we encounter views that challenge our understanding of the world, our advantages, or our biases. Because, after all, good people are not supposed to be biased. Good people are not supposed to benefit from privilege. The views of good people should take priority over others. Good people are not defensive and never cause harm. Allow for a moment of redirection: this is not reality. Being good does not mean being perfect. Say it aloud - "Being good does not mean being perfect."

Goodness is a moment captured. We all have the capacity to be good in a moment, just as much as we all have the capacity to not be good in another moment. As I remix the words of Jim Collins from his book Good to Great, I believe "good is the enemy of better." True goodness is not about maintaining the status quo nor is it returning to the past. True goodness is a commitment to becoming better in those moments. We should intentionally work towards becoming better, however becoming better does not happen without discomfort.

Human beings have a strong desire for comfort, and many of us will do all we can to avoid discomfort. A certain element of discomfort is inherently embedded within human nature. It's why infants cry when they're hungry or have a dirty diaper. This biological mechanism helps protect our well-being and safety. There is another component of discomfort that is developed through our environment and experiences. It can be defined as acquired. This aspect of discomfort causes human beings to gravitate towards the familiar, the effortless, and the self-preserving. Much of human belief, behavior, and identity is shaped by environmental factors and early life experiences. An individual's identity is significantly shaped by the influence of loved ones whom we regard as positive role models. Throughout this developmental process, values are assigned to beliefs and actions, often categorizing them as either beneficial or detrimental. When a belief or action conflicts with our own beliefs or responses, it can make us uncomfortable, especially if it challenges our sense of being right or justified. Science has demonstrated that, when individuals perceive a threat, they typically exhibit fight, flight, or freeze responses. Although discomfort arising from difference may not initially present itself through visible fight, flight, or freeze behaviors, it nonetheless influences us significantly. For many people, such reactions often occurs unconsciously at emotional and psychological levels. While discomfort is often viewed as something to avoid, it is the gateway to transformation. When embraced, discomfort becomes less intimidating and more empowering.

My Personal Story of Embracing the Discomfort of Difference

As we move forward in this book, I am going to share something that's not theoretical or conceptual, but deeply personal. This part of the book isn't a framework, a strategy, or a step-by-step guide. It's my personal story.

It's one thing to talk about embracing the discomfort of difference in the abstract, but it's another thing to actually live it. To sit across the table from someone whose worldview challenges yours. To listen when it would be easier to walk away. To stay in tension when your instincts say to retreat. To be vulnerable, misunderstood, or even wrong, and still choose to lean in. That's what this section is about.

It's about my journey navigating a difference of identity that is deeply connected to my faith. It's about conversations I never planned to have but needed to. The people I never expected to grow with but ultimately couldn't grow without. You'll see that embracing difference isn't about abandoning who you are. Embracing difference is about being courageous enough to let who you are become stretched and shaped by meaningful connection. You'll also see that discomfort isn't the enemy. It's the signal that something real is happening, worth paying attention to, and quite possibly enriches your life more than you can imagine.

So, I invite you into this part of my journey - not because it's perfect, but because it's honest. And in the honesty, I hope you'll see the very heartbeat of Better Together come to life.

The year 2000 was a significant year for me. I began a new life with my wife, Kimberly. Although I had some ideas that my life would change, I did not understand the full extent of how I might be challenged to evolve. One such moment arose when my wife addressed me in how I treated men who identified with the LGBTQ+ Community. She noticed that I greeted and spoke with these individuals differently than I did with men that I believed were heterosexuals. My wife knew that I desired to be a good person and that I intentionally put forth effort to be a good person. She also believed there was an opportunity for me to be better. Her courage to "call me up" in my perspective and in my behavior created discomfort within me. This discomfort felt like an indictment to my effort and desire to be a good person. This perceived indictment caused me to initially focus on defending myself and my goodness. I personally used God to justify my prejudiced jokes, my biased behavior, and my fixed mindset, in an effort to protect my comfort. My comfort was founded in what I had been taught and what I had come to live by without a well-rounded understanding.

As I began to wrestle with my discomfort, I realized it was an invitation. An invitation for me to explore who I was. Who I really was? An invitation to understand what I believe and why I believe what I believe. It was also an invitation for me to become a better version of myself.

Comfort to Discomfort
Key Points

◈ Being good is not simply defined as right/wrong or good/ bad.

◈ Discomfort is not an indictment but an invitation.

◈ True goodness is found in the pursuit of better even if better is uncomfortable.

◈ Exercise: Recall a time when you faced discomfort but emerged stronger. Write about what you learned and how it reshaped your perspective.

The Stretch That Shapes

"When we strive to become better than we are, everything around us becomes better too."
— Paulo Coelho (The Alchemist)

After our discussion on the tensions sparked by the deaths of Philando Castile and Alton Sterling, I heard from attendees who continued the conversation that some met for coffee while others hosted dinners. Inspired, I began posting on social media to encourage more dialogue, hoping even virtual spaces could foster growth through discomfort. Though I'm naturally conflict averse, I realized both I and others needed to embrace this temporary unease to truly grow.

A lot of people talk about continuous improvement, personal development, and personal growth - becoming a better version of themselves. I'm not sure how many people are actually willing to experience the discomfort that comes along with significant growth. Growth is rarely smooth or comfortable, even from an individual, personal perspective. It becomes even more challenging and complicated when we consider relational growth.

It often disrupts routines, pushes boundaries, and challenges long-held beliefs. As stated before, human beings instinctively resist discomfort because it feels like a threat. Realistically, discomfort is a sign that something new is being formed. Discomfort can be a doorway to not only improvement but transformation.

The human brain is a true wonder. It can remember, recognize, control, and process, but even more impressively, it can change and adapt. This ability to change through experience is called neuroplasticity, and it thrives on challenge and discomfort. Now, let me say that again like I'm preaching on a Sunday morning: The brain's ability to change thrives on challenge and discomfort!

When we face challenges and lean into discomfort, our neural pathways stretch. That discomfort doesn't just make us squirm. Discomfort can reshape the brain, forming new connections and making room for new perspectives. Okay, here comes the nerdy side of me. Once our brains experience that stretch and growth, they crave more of it. Why? Because the brain rewards us for leaning into discomfort and forming new connections by releasing dopamine - the feel-good chemical. Dopamine is part of the brain's reward system. It kicks in when we accomplish something meaningful or make an emotional connection. So, when you push through discomfort and grow, your brain basically throws you a little party. That dopamine hit reinforces that the stretch was worth it and makes you more likely to seek out growth again.

Engaging in a conversation with someone who holds a different belief can present a challenge. The stretch from the conversation can help you develop empathy for someone who you might naturally have a hard time having empathy for. The stretch can be having someone choosing to call you up. Being called up is when someone is inviting you to reflect on how your words or actions might be offensive or harmful. While being called up can feel uncomfortable, it's far more constructive than being called out, which often leads to defensiveness and division.

Whatever form the stretch takes, when you embrace the discomfort that comes with it, your brain rewards you. Literally. It releases dopamine - the chemical that makes you feel good - reinforcing that the stretch was worth it. Over time, these moments begin to rewire your brain and reshape your mindset. Without a good stretch your mindset tends to remain fixed. Mindset matters and is critical to how people approach challenges and even the perception of discomfort. Psychologist Carol Dweck, whose research has deeply influenced my thinking, describes a fixed mindset as the belief that core qualities are innate and unchangeable, while a growth mindset reflects the belief that these qualities can be developed through effort, deliberate practice, and persistence (Dweck, 2006).I've never been accused of being profound, but here's something I believe deeply: a fixed mindset doesn't have to stay fixed. It takes just as much energy to stay stuck as it does to stretch and grow.

Every day, we're presented with opportunities to choose between comfort and growth. These daily opportunities can be both obvious and subtle. Most of us don't recognize these moments for what they are: decisions to remain the same or to become better. The choice is yours.

Choosing to stretch and grow isn't just a personal decision, it's a relational one. Our choices ripple outward. When you embrace the discomfort that comes with growing your awareness, empathy, and courage, you don't just change yourself but you influence your relationships, your teams, and your communities. Personal growth fuels communal growth. When you become better, your family benefits. Your workplace becomes stronger. Your spiritual community deepens. Your willingness to grow doesn't just shape your life. It shapes and reshapes your circle of influence. Growth is never passive. It demands effort, risk, and yes, discomfort. But every step toward growth is a step toward something greater. Because a commitment to growth is, at its core, a commitment to discomfort.

My Personal Story of Embracing the Discomfort of Difference

In my journey to become a better version of myself, I had to confront a hard truth: I held biases and had discriminated against members of the LGBTQ+ community. Acknowledging this was both challenging and deeply uncomfortable. For much of my life, I mistreated, disrespected, and even demonized what I didn't understand, especially when it came to people whose identities differed from what I had been taught to accept. I used my faith and the Word of God as a shield to avoid the discomfort of engaging with those who were different. Eventually, I found myself at a crossroads. I could either stay rooted in what was familiar and comfortable, or I could begin the difficult but necessary work of becoming better.

Wrestling with beliefs I had held my entire life was emotionally and mentally exhausting. The discomfort stretched me in ways that made me want to give up more than once.

I'm not naturally the most disciplined person, but my desire to grow - to truly become better - has often been stronger than the pull of temporary comfort. I've come to accept that on the other side of discomfort is transformation. And that transformation doesn't just change me, but it has the potential to ripple outward and make others better too.

The Stretch That Shapes Key Points

◈ Discomfort can lead to transformation.

◈ The brain is wired to reward stretch.

◈ Mindset determines your capacity to grow.

◈ Exercise: Identify one area where you want to grow. Outline three specific actions you can take, even if they make you uncomfortable. Challenge yourself to practice one of these actions for 21 consecutive days.

When Discomfort Turns to Conflict

***"The truth will set you free, but first it will make you uncomfortable."* – James Baldwin**

From 2006 to 2016, my family attended a multicultural church. Based on my observation, the congregation was approximately 60% white, 35% Black, and 5% other ethnicities. We were proud of who we were. A Christian church in the heart of the Bible Belt that reflected diversity not just in attendance, but in leadership as well. For a church of over 1,000 members, that level of diversity, both in the pews and on the platform, felt like a glimpse of heaven. We shared a common understanding of Scripture, the Holy Sacraments, and even worship music. Yes, there were differences but we had learned to navigate them for the good of the Kingdom.

Then came the deaths of Philando Castile and Alton Sterling. These tragedies tested the peaceful and impartial nature of our fellowship. From my perspective, to maintain unity, the church said very little, if anything, about what was happening in our country and in our community. I believe that silence was a missed opportunity. The church could have leaned into the discomfort, even if it meant facing some healthy conflict. Growth doesn't come from avoiding hard conversations. It comes from engaging them with courage and compassion.

Discomfort can take on various forms. Sometimes it's a quiet internal stirring. A question that won't go away. A tension between you and a colleague. A conversation that lingers long after it has ended. The discomfort turns into tension, and the tension turns into conflict. When we encounter differences – a new idea, a cultural perspective, a challenge to our beliefs, an opinion of right versus wrong – our instinctive response is to protect what feels safe. That instinct is rooted in self-preservation. As referenced before our brains are wired to defend what we believe and thus who we are or hope to be. So, when someone challenges our worldview, it can feel like they are challenging our worth.

What looks like disagreement on the surface is often a reflection of something more personal underneath. What is underneath can stir up fear, pain, pride, shame, grief, etc.. Disagreement can activate these emotional undercurrents: the fear of being misunderstood, the pain of past rejection, the pride of not being right, the shame of not being seen, and the grief of not being validated. So, when disagreement turns into conflict, it's rarely about the issue at hand but more about the meaning – identity, power, belonging. Conflict is not the problem. Unresolved, mismanaged, and avoided conflict is the problem. It is important for us to realize that the conflict is carrying a deeper story.

I think it is important for us to recognize the difference between a stretch and conflict. The stretch, as described earlier, is often an internal process - an invitation to grow, reflect, and expand our understanding. Conflict, on the other hand, is the friction between people when values, experiences and perceptions collide. It can be painful. It can leave bruises. It not only forces us to confront what we believe but also challenges how we show up in the presence of someone who believes differently. In conflict, the stakes often feel higher. Emotions rise. Defenses go up. And when that moment comes, we typically respond in a few predictable ways.

A common response to conflict is avoidance. Avoidance can come in different forms. It can be deflecting or changing the subject. It can be nodding in agreement just to keep the peace. Ghosting conversations or relationships is a common form of avoidance. Another way we avoid conflict is by telling ourselves, “It’s just not worth it. Avoidance is a way we protect ourselves. I suggest avoidance is based on fear – saying the wrong thing, being misunderstood, or rocking the boat. Avoidance might feel like keeping the peace, but often leads to disconnection, reinforces echo chambers, and prevents us from learning about others and ourselves.

Another response to conflict is aggression. Aggression shows up as our fear is magnified in the form of a personal loss – loss of power, status, identity, or certainty. When who we are or what we believe is threatened, we will fight back to safeguard what we know and believe. Aggression can show up as being defensive or dismissive. It will cause you to talk over others to assert your viewpoint. Another form of aggression that I had a hard time overcoming is sarcasm. Lastly, I suggest that stubbornness is another form of aggression. When we are aggressive in our responses it can shut down conversations and create emotional harm. It can widen the gap between people and reduce the opportunity for transparent and transformative dialogue.

The response to conflict that I would like to uplift is engaging with curiosity. This response reflects emotional maturity and a growth mindset. When we respond with curiosity it shows that conflict is not the enemy. Engagement with curiosity comes from the belief that understanding differences helps us become better together. Engagement with curiosity involves asking thoughtful questions to better understand another person's experience. It can be as simple as admitting that you do not know something. It is also good to acknowledge that tension will happen but deciding to lean in with humility when it happens rather than hostility is better. Curiosity turns conflict into possibility. It builds trust, deepens relationships, and expands worldviews. Expanding a worldview does not mean that a world- view has to change. Curiosity shows that you care more about connection than you do comfort.

When Discomfort Turns to Conflict ***Key Points***

◈ Name the discomfort before it becomes destructive.

◈ Conflict is not inherently negative.

◈ Choose curiosity over certainty.

◈ Exercise: Think of a time you felt uncomfortable during a disagreement with someone. Acknowledge your behavior: avoidance, aggression, or engagement with curiosity. What made you uncomfortable? How could you have responded differently? Practice asking curious questions for your next un- comfortable conversation (because it is coming).

Discovering the Beauty of Difference

***"Isn't it amazing that we are all made in God's image, and yet there is so much diversity among his people."* - Desmond Tutu**

2016 was a game-changer for me. Even the night before it began hinted at the journey I was about to embark on. On December 31, 2015, while preparing for the Davis Family New Year's Eve Party, I left the house to run a few errands. As I pulled out of the neighborhood, I found myself behind a truck flying a Con- federate flag. My first reaction was, "Still?" I tried to brush it off, but as the truck kept making the same turns I did - intersection after intersection - my frustration grew. At a red light, I snapped a photo of the flag. Eventually, we ended up in the same parking lot. I parked, uploaded the photo to social media, and went into the store. Twenty minutes later, I returned to my car and was stunned by the number of comments. The post had sparked a wide range of reactions. Some thoughtful.

Some heated. Some that made me question whether I had helped or hurt the conversation.

As someone who feels a calling to bring people together, I immediately began to feel a deep sense of guilt. The comment section had become a battleground, and I wasn't proud of what I had unintentionally ignited. So, I decided to do something different. I invited anyone who had commented - regardless of their perspective - to meet in person and talk. About eleven people showed up. Two of them, whom I respected deeply, held very different views from mine about the flag. I don't know if anyone's mind was changed that night, but that conversation marked a turning point for me. It was the moment I began to truly discover the beauty of difference.

Difference invites us to move beyond sameness and step into a space where deeper understanding, creativity, and complexity can thrive. It challenges our assumptions, stretches our thinking, and reveals the limits of a single viewpoint. When we encounter differences, whether in culture, background, thought, or lived experience, we are pushed to expand our worldview. We are encouraged to ask better questions, listen more intentionally, and reflect more honestly.

Difference is often viewed through a narrow lens. It is often seen as something to manage, tolerate, or politely work around. But what if we saw it differently? What if difference wasn't a problem to solve, but a gift to explore? Rather than seeing difference as something to fix, imagine reframing difference as something beautiful to discover, appreciate, and be transformed by. Difference spans the full range of human distinctions: race, gender, background, identity, age, culture, thought process, ability, personality, and so much more. But it's not just a label or a checkbox. It's a lived experience. One that shapes how people see the world. The difference of an individual can impact how they experience life, and how they interact with others.

Too often, we reduce difference to checkboxes or surface-level diversity. But true difference lives in the stories people carry - the challenges they've overcome, the perspectives they've gained, and the lenses through which they view life. In our LIFT training at UpLift Coaching & Consulting, we use an activity called the Identity Iceberg. It encourages individuals to share parts of themselves that lie beneath the surface, beyond job titles, roles, or appearances. Time and again, we've seen that when someone has the courage to be open and vulnerable - sharing their experiences, struggles, or fears - it's met not with judgment, but with empathy, understanding, and support. Discovering the beauty of difference begins with listening to those stories. When we avoid, erase, or dismiss someone's lived experience simply because it's different from our own, we not only harm the person who lived it, but we also rob ourselves of the opportunity to grow.

Difference, even in the name of diversity, is not just about representation; it's about the richness that comes from varied experiences, perspectives, and backgrounds. The presence of difference challenges us to think bigger and broader. Diversity introduces unfamiliar viewpoints that may disrupt our comfort but also stretch our capacity. In diverse communities and teams, ideas are refined, solutions are strengthened, and innovation is accelerated because difference sharpens us. When we lean into our differences rather than withdraw, we discover that we are better thinkers, better problem-solvers, and better people because of it.

My Personal Story of Embracing the Discomfort of Difference

As my journey continued, I recognized that I did not have a significant relationship with anyone who identified as a member of the LGBTQ Community. I was trying to understand a different perspective, but it felt like I was pressing the gas pedal with my brain in drive, only to discover the car was sitting on cinder blocks with no tires. I was burning energy but going nowhere. I found myself thinking about something that I had no life experience about. Or I would talk with another friend who believed what I believed or something very similar. So, there I was again revving the engine, wheels spinning, but stuck in place. A colleague of mine, Dan, once said something that stuck with me: "You can't fix what's in your head with what's in your head." I call that "simply profound." As a heterosexual, southern, Pentecostal Christian male raised in rural Arkansas, I was trying to understand what it meant to be a member of the LGBTQ+ Community - on my own, or at best, with others who knew as little as I did.

At some point, I decided to lean in more with an honest assessment of myself. I acknowledged that as a black man I intentionally spent time with white friends and colleagues so that they might have a better understanding and knowledge of what it means to be a black person in America. In these moments together, I would like to believe that we learned from each other and gained new insights from each other personally as well as culturally. It is in that moment I realized that for me to demolish some biases that I had about the LGBTQ+ Community while developing my understanding, I would have to get out of my own head. I knew I specifically needed to spend time with a man who identified as gay.

After thinking through the men I knew who were openly gay and building up the courage, I reached out to a colleague, Courtney Robertson, and asked if he'd be willing to grab lunch. He accepted. Sitting across from him at the table, I was as nervous as I'd ever been. I did not know how to tell him about my past mindset and behavior towards the LGBTQ+ community. I didn't know how to say that I wanted to better understand someone who was gay or ask if he'd be willing to help me learn. I worried he might be offended, or even righteously angry. But at some point, I opened my mouth, and words started to come out. I don't even remember exactly what I said but I know the words came from my heart. To my thankful and welcome surprise, his response was one of the most beautiful and memorable moments of my life. He met me right where I was. He welcomed me into his life. He allowed me to grow in my understanding and supported me even through my ignorance.

Discovering the Beauty of Difference ***Key Points***

◈ There are tangible benefits to having differences in communities and workplaces.

◈ Reframe and reimagine differences as beautiful and worth pursuing.

◈ Ignoring what is different is a missed opportunity.

◈ Exercise: Think about a diverse group you are part of. Reflect on how the differences within the group have strengthened it.

Seeking & Understanding Difference

***"Too often we... enjoy the comfort of opinion without the discomfort of thought."* - John F. Kennedy**

A post I shared on social media opened the door to conversations with people who held different perspectives - conversations that ultimately led me to seek deeper understanding of our differences. I was able to meet with individuals one-on-one, couple-to-couple, or even with groups that ranged from 6 to 25 individuals. Through these conversations I was able to learn more about the other person(s) while also learning more about myself. I believe in many cases the other individuals grew as well.

The journey of seeking and understanding differences - whether in experience, behavior, thought, culture, or belief - will most likely be a journey of discomfort. The journey to embrace the discomfort of difference is a refining process. In the Book of

Proverbs it says, "As iron sharpens iron, so one person sharpens another" (Proverbs 27:17, NIV). I often thought of this in terms of people who already have established relationships. These individuals most likely have much in common and they are willing to hold each other accountable with a desire to make each other better. I have experienced this personally and still hold this to be true. What I have also come to learn is I have experienced the most growth when I have engaged with individuals where a difference between us was significant. In either situation, "iron sharpening iron" highlights both the benefits and the tension of growth. There are pros and cons of seeking and understanding differences.

When one piece of iron, the blade of a knife, is rubbed against another piece of iron, such as a file, the friction between the two surfaces removes small bits of metal from the blade. This friction sharpens the edge, making it better and more effective for its purpose. Just as iron needs friction to sharpen, people need discomfort to become better. Being around others who think differently can make you better. Spending time with those who question your assumptions can make you better. Engaging with people who push you beyond your limits can make you better. Sharpening is productive, but it is not always pleasant.

Depending on the force and speed, the friction may generate heat or sparks, symbolizing the intensity of the process. The heat isn't a sign of damage, but a visible expression of the transformation that is taking place to the iron. In human beings, difficult conversations and moments of vulnerability often come with emotional intensity. While the heat and sparks created may be a sign of discomfort, it can also be a signal that something very meaningful is happening. This is not a sign to retreat but to lean in. This is an opportunity to lean into the refining process of becoming more aware of yourself as well as others.

Effective sharpening isn’t just about brute force. It requires control, care, and consistency. If rushed or mishandled, sharpening can damage the blade. Done properly, it results in a refined and improved tool. Growth through relationships doesn't happen automatically. It takes intentional listening, feedback, truth-telling, and mutual respect. When navigating differences, emotional control is essential. Sharpening isn’t always a linear path. Sometimes you might use too much force or mishandle a situation, but that does not mean the blade is ruined. Some situations might require more control, care and consistency to re- fine and strengthen the blade to be stronger than it was before.

When we disagree or feel challenged, it is common to react impulsively or defensively. Intentional listening, the practice of hearing to understand, not just to respond, will help you to approach conversations without the intent to “win” but with the purpose of becoming better together. Care is shown through respecting the integrity of the blade. We show care by recognizing the value and dignity of the other person and not trying to reshape them. Sharpening is not redesigning. Blades dull with use and require consistent maintenance. The consistency to show up with empathy, awareness, and a growth mindset strengthens trust while developing a deeper connection even in the midst of differences.

The ultimate goal of “iron sharpening iron” in this journey of seeking and understanding differences is mutual transformation. In the process of sharpening iron, neither piece remains unchanged. Likewise, when two people who have differences engage with empathy, honesty, vulnerability, intent, and openness, they each walk away changed. Change isn't always immediate or easy to recognize, but that doesn't mean it isn't happening. Growth often works quietly, beneath the surface. And that's why consistency matters.

To shift the metaphor for a moment: it's like building muscle. Muscles grow under tension and so do minds and hearts. It's the steady, repeated engagement with discomfort that creates sustained development. Through every tension-filled conversation, every moment of listening, and every choice to stay in a relationship despite our differences, we become better together.

My Personal Story of Embracing the Discomfort of Difference

Courtney, who helped me to embrace my own discomfort around sexual orientation, is no longer just a colleague, but a true friend and brother. I know that I am a better person because of him, and I hope that I have enhanced his life as much as he has enhanced mine. Even with the amazing relationship I have with my friend, his partner, and my wife, the discomfort didn't disappear. It simply shifted. As I was growing in my understanding and perspective of the LGBTQ+ Community, not everyone in my life was on the same journey. Although my awareness of someone else's lived experience was expanding, I did not have enough confidence to share what I was learning and how my feelings and perspectives were shifting. I was becoming uncomfortable now around friends and family who were doing the things I used to do and speak. A homophobic joke wasn't just a joke anymore. That joke now had a name and a face, and for me it was of someone who I care about.

Too often when human beings' eyes come open to truth, we are too willing to damage those who are now guilty of the very thing we used to do. I knew that I wanted to bring others along with me, but it was going to take time, care, and consistency. During my time with an organization called Young Life, I learned a powerful principle: "You earn the right to be heard." And as Soup Campbell, an incredible minister and human being, once said, "More is caught than taught." Both of these truths have shaped how I approach relationships, influence, and growth. The sharpening that I still needed and wanted to provide for others was going to happen through my consistent actions – not telling jokes, not laughing at jokes, but openly engaging and embracing members of the LGBTQ+ Community.

Seeking and Understanding Difference ***Key Points***

◇ Discomfort is often a signal that sharpening is underway.

◇ Sharpening is not a one-sided process.

◇ The sharpening process requires control, care, and consistency.

◇ Exercise: Choose one person in your life who is different from you in a significant way. Schedule a conversation with them to learn about their experiences and perspectives.

Reflections For This Exercise:

- It doesn't have to be someone you disagree with but consider someone whose life experiences challenges your comfort zone or assumptions.
- Approach with curiosity and not an agenda.

- Use a simple and respectful approach with someone you have a relationship with.
- Avoid anything that feels like an interrogation.

Better Together - Uniting Through Difference

"Strength lies in differences, not in similarities."
- Stephen R. Covey

One of the individuals who accepted my invitation to engage in conversation following the deaths of Alton Sterling and Philando Castile was Mark Davis. Mark and I met at our daughters' school. Mark is a white man from a blue-collar, working-class family in Ohio. We quickly noticed that we had few common interests beyond being "Girl Dads". Due to these common threads, we started meeting outside of school events primarily connected to sports. I was pleased to see Mark at the conversation and even more thrilled to see our conversations evolve after that evening. Our interactions started to move beyond the usual safe topics - sports, family, school routines - and into more meaningful territory.

We moved beyond easy conversations and began leaning

into the complex, often uncomfortable topics of life: politics, religion, human equity, and more. Let me remind you, this was 2016, a year marked by one of the most controversial and openly divisive presidential elections I had experienced up to that point. Mark and I began to explore the differences in our lives. Some were small differences that didn't threaten our relationship. Others were more significant, the kind that had historically disrupted or even ended relationships in my past. And yet, we navigated those conversations with honesty and respect. We didn't avoid our differences. We embraced them. And in doing so, we strengthened our connection.

Then an unforgettable day happened. We met up for lunch one day at a Downtown Memphis restaurant. At some point, during the conversation, the topic of "white privilege" came up. I spoke about the existence of white privilege and how much of a challenge it is for me but more specifically for people of color in America. Mark pushed back and I would say primarily from a personal perspective. He shared that he had come from a family where nothing was given to them and that they worked hard for everything they earned and achieved. I didn't disagree with those points and affirmed that even with that being true, being white in America provides a person with benefits that are often unconscious, unspoken, invisible, and not always measurable.

This was probably the most uncomfortable conversation that Mark and I had at this point in our relationship. As we parted ways, and I sat alone in my car, I remember thinking, "This might be the beginning of the end." It has been these types of uncomfortable conversations where someone and I express a difference of opinion on a subject that can lead to a chasm in that relationship. I was so grateful to find out that Mark was not deterred by our difference but may have become more curious.

We continued to meet. We continued to engage. We continued to share. We continued to ask each other questions. We leaned into our differences and embraced the discomfort.

In a later conversation, we spoke about our sixteen-year-old daughters who were both learning how to drive. All the typical parenting talk of your first child driving: anxiety of your child driving in the city, the disappointment of increased auto insurance cost, the inability to sleep at night until they make it home, and the frustration of having to have "the talk." Mark asked me what I was referring to. I shared with him that it's the talk that every parent of a black or brown child in America should have with their child about what to do when stopped and/or addressed by a state-sanctioned officer. Mark wondered if that was necessary for me and my family. After all, my daughter was in the same private school his daughter attended, we lived in the suburbs, and our family was well-respected in the community. I told Mark that it was not a talk that I wanted to have but it was a talk that I believed I had to have. Mark called me weeks later to apologize for denying the existence of white privilege. I was not expecting an apology from him about his perspective on this topic nor did I feel like I needed one, but as he explained his why, I felt so connected to him. Mark shared that after our conversation about "the talk," he couldn't stop thinking about why I felt so strongly about preparing my daughter for interactions with the police. He shared that he came to the realization that he never had that talk with his daughter because he didn't need to. Mark acknowledged that he started to understand that having advantages doesn't mean that everything was handed to him nor does it mean that he didn't work hard.

Mark's willingness to keep an open mind, remain curious, and stay engaged gave me hope not only for our relationship but for humanity. It reignited my belief that, as human beings, we have the capacity to work through our differences. It was a reaffirmation of what I have long felt about the capacity of humanity to evolve within a realm of selflessness. It's easy to evolve when there is a direct benefit for evolving. The challenge is choosing to consider another perspective, idea, belief, or action when someone else appears to be the beneficiary of the evolved state. Self-preservation is a natural response for human beings and is often used to protect us from harm. Self-preservation in the form of perceived loss, failure, embarrassment, or lack of effort becomes an obstacle for growth, development, and ultimately unity. Unity can come in the form of unison, but it can also come in the form of harmony.

When I was in high school band, there were times when all the trumpets played the exact same note. That was unity expressed through unison - clear, powerful, and in sync. But more often, our parts required us to play different notes. That was unity expressed through harmony. Three trumpets, three distinct notes, coming together to create a sound that was richer and fuller than any single note could produce. Harmony honors difference without creating division. It's not about everyone being the same. It's about everyone contributing their unique voice to something greater. Mark and I were learning to harmonize together. We both had a goal of unity and not uniformity. We begin to honor the value of our differences and explore opportunities to further develop each other. In 2019, Mark called to let me know he had recommended me as someone who could potentially support the leadership team of a division within his company, where he served as a manager. I was not looking for a job and asked him why. He told me that his company was focused on enhancing their culture. The company wanted every single member of their organization to feel a deep sense of belonging and value. Mark thought that I was the perfect person to support their team. After getting over my shock, I agreed to meet with the leadership team and discuss their challenges as well as their goals.

That initial meeting led to another, and then another with each one deepening the conversation. Eventually, those discussions opened the door to a meeting with someone at the Corporate Home Office. That opportunity ultimately led Kim and me to start our own business, UpLift Coaching & Consulting. Through this business, we now encourage others to do what Mark and I started over 10 years ago - a willingness to engage with and explore individuals who may be different than you. We encourage people to lean into the courage that is required to embrace the discomfort that comes along with our differences.

Mark and I have learned that we are better together even amid our differences. Our differences have stretched us and made us better. While our differences have made us uncomfortable at times, they've also made us better. Our differences have challenged us individually and collectively, but they've also made us better. We could have chosen to isolate ourselves, allowing those differences to reinforce our own beliefs and biases, limit our emotional capacity, and rob us of meaningful human connections. Instead, we chose to lean in. And because we did, we discovered that unity isn't the absence of difference. Unity is the decision to honor one another despite it.

When we embrace differences, we create spaces where every person's unique contribution is valued. That kind of unity, born through difference, is exactly what makes us Better Together.

Uniting Through Differences ***Key Points***

◈ Growth begins in our transparency and vulnerability.

◈ Seek understanding even amid disagreement.

◈ Unity is not sameness, but a commitment to harmony.

◈ Exercise: Identify a project or goal you are working on. Reflect on how incorporating diverse perspectives could enhance the outcome.

Conclusion: Embracing the Journey

Being "better together" isn't about surface-level diversity or performative inclusion. It's about doing the hard work of showing up, staying in the room, and embracing people whose stories, struggles, and truths look nothing like yours. When we unite through difference, we build something bigger than tolerance. We build belonging. Tolerance is passive. Belonging is active. Tolerance can look like quiet distance, polite silence, or "putting up with" someone. Belonging can look like shared effort, emotional investment, or a willingness to stay in a conversation even when it's uncomfortable. Tolerance says, "I'll make room for you, as long as you don't disrupt my comfort." Belonging says, "You're fully welcome here, even when your presence stretches me."

Being "better together" does not require agreement but it does require commitment. A commitment that is greater than the comfort of sameness. A commitment to choose curiosity instead of judgment. A commitment to authentically see and hear someone with a different perspective or experience. A commitment to disagree with another person without dismissing them. A commitment to providing a safe space for every person.

Being "better together" is not just about getting by, holding us together, or keeping us from falling apart. Being "better together" calls us to grow, stretch, and evolve through our similarities as well as our differences. Being "better together" does not erase our differences but invites us to bring our full selves into relationships while encouraging others to do the same. Being "better together" requires us to create a space where we challenge one another respectfully, confront our assumptions with humility, and stay committed even when the conversation gets hard.

Embracing different perspectives sharpens our own ideas. Exposing ourselves to different lived experiences deepens our empathy. Engaging in uncomfortable conversations with grace expands our capacity for collaboration. Difference and discomfort are not barriers; they are opportunities. When we lean into the discomfort of difference, the potential to create homes, communities, and workplaces with better thinkers, better listeners, better teammates, better people who are better together. The journey won't always be easy, but it will always be worth it.

Reality Check

After the deaths of George Floyd and Breonna Taylor in 2020, I sent an invitation through a social media platform for those who were emotionally and psychologically hurting to join me in a virtual space. The intention was to bring people into a safe space to discuss what they were feeling and experiencing. While I wanted to create a safe space for individuals who were frustrated, I also attempted to allow space for individuals whose feelings and perspectives were different. One of the participants had different feelings about the state sanctioned officers in both the Floyd and Taylor deaths The energy in the space shifted from feeling safe to feeling tense when one participant began to challenge and question the thoughts of others. One of my biggest regrets is how I failed to navigate that moment more effectively. In my effort to create a space for growth and understanding, I recognize that some participants left feeling more hurt and frustrated than when they arrived.

Growth requires discomfort but discomfort does not mean danger. And difference is not an excuse for disrespect. Embracing difference is not the same as accepting disrespect. Seeking understanding does not require sacrificing dignity. Extending grace does not mean excusing harm. We lean into discomfort not to be consumed by it, but to be changed by it. We stay at the table not to be diminished but to contribute. We continue to engage not to defeat but to listen. We commit to challenging others while being challenged by others. The pursuit of embracing difference does not mean allowing yourself or others to be disrespected or abused. Even as we are embracing the discomfort of difference, we must protect our peace and defend the safety of others.

Call to Action:

How will you step into discomfort to grow? How will you seek and celebrate differences in your life? Write down your commitment and revisit it regularly.

References

Biblica, Inc. (2011). Holy Bible, New International Version.

Collins, J. (2001). Good to great: Why some companies make the leap... and others don't. Harper Business.

Covey, Stephen (n.d.). Strength lies in differences, not in similarities. [Quote].

Dweck, C. S. (2006). Mindset: The new psychology of success. Random House.

Kennedy, J. F. (n.d.). Too often we enjoy the comfort of opinion without the discomfort of thought. [Quote].

Reagan, Ronald (n.d.). Peace is not the absence of conflict, but the ability to cope with it. [Quote].

Tutu, D. (n.d.). Isn't it amazing that we are all made in God's image, and yet there is so much diversity among his people. [Quote].

Majors, J. (n.d.). Growth is uncomfortable; you have to embrace the discomfort if you want to expand. [Quote].

Goggins, D. (n.d.). Our whole life is set up in the path of least resistance… So the whole time, we're living our lives in a very comfortable area. There's no growth in that. [Quote].

Index

Made in the USA
Coppell, TX
20 February 2026

71853773R00046